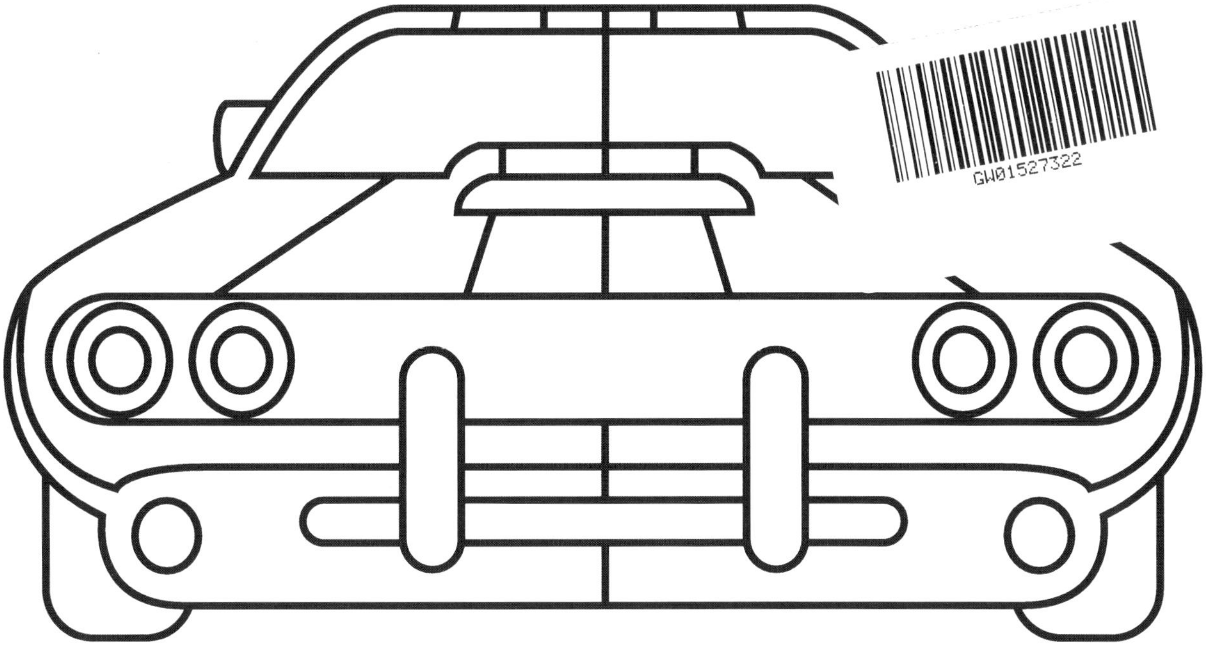

SUPERCAR COLORING BOOK

THIS BOOK

BELONGS TO:

....

COLOR TEST PAGE

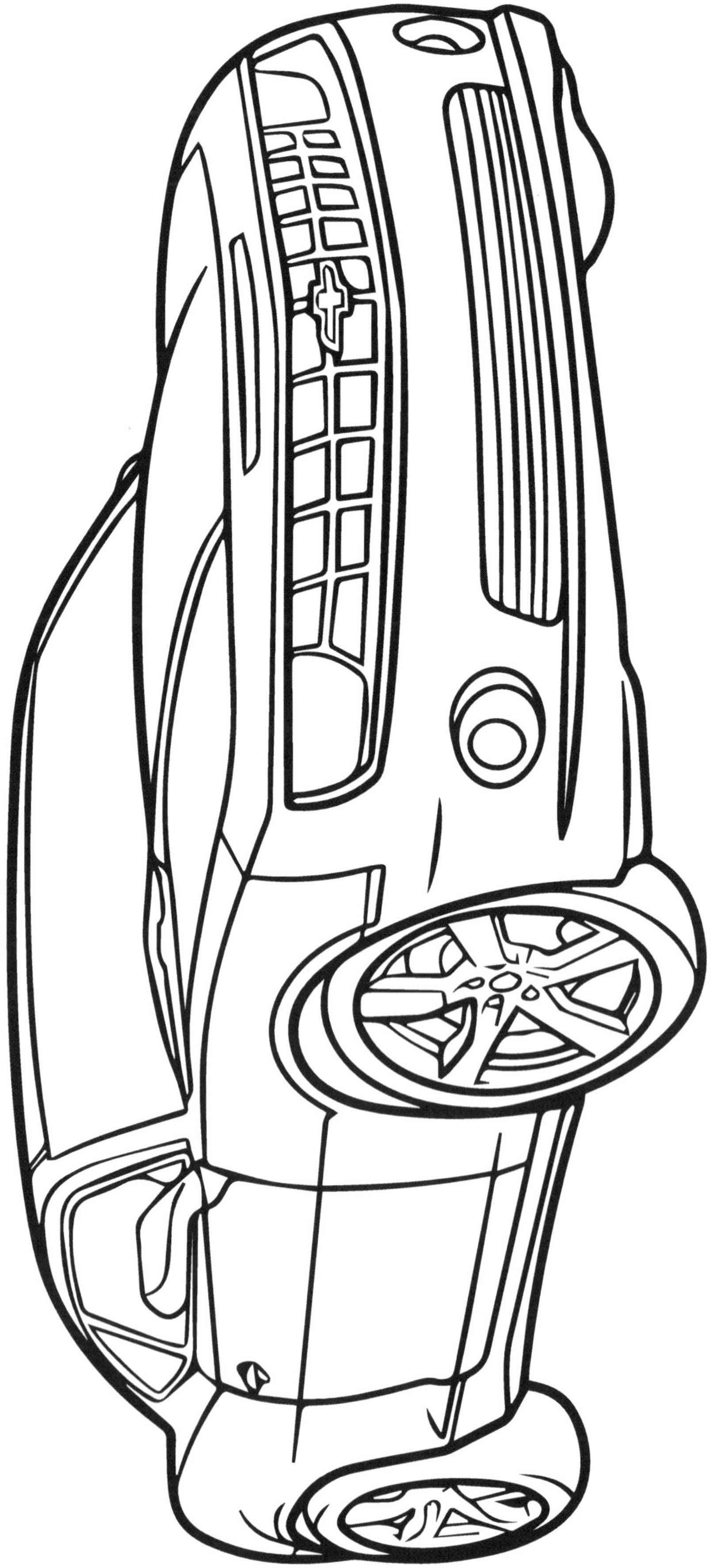

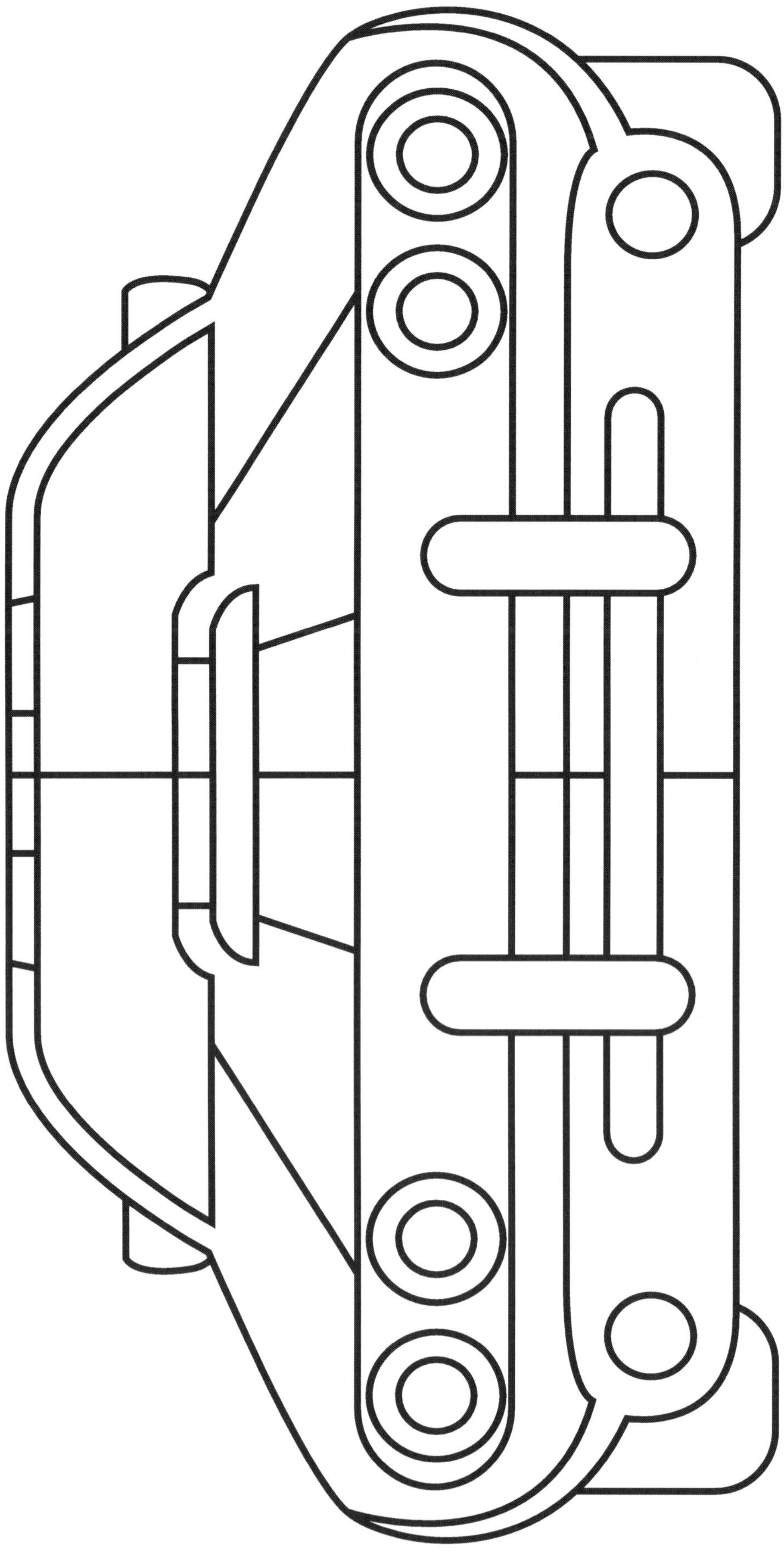

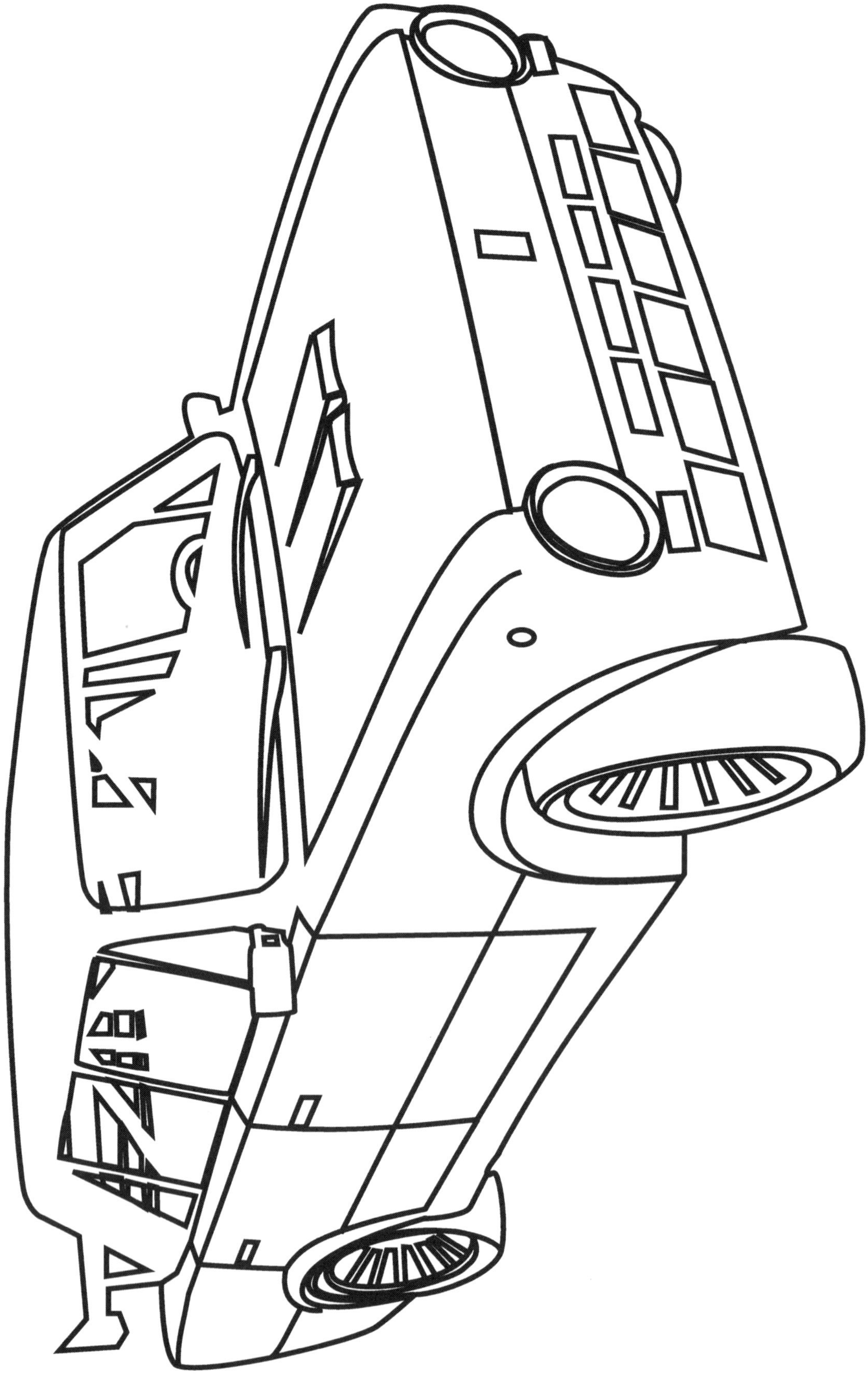

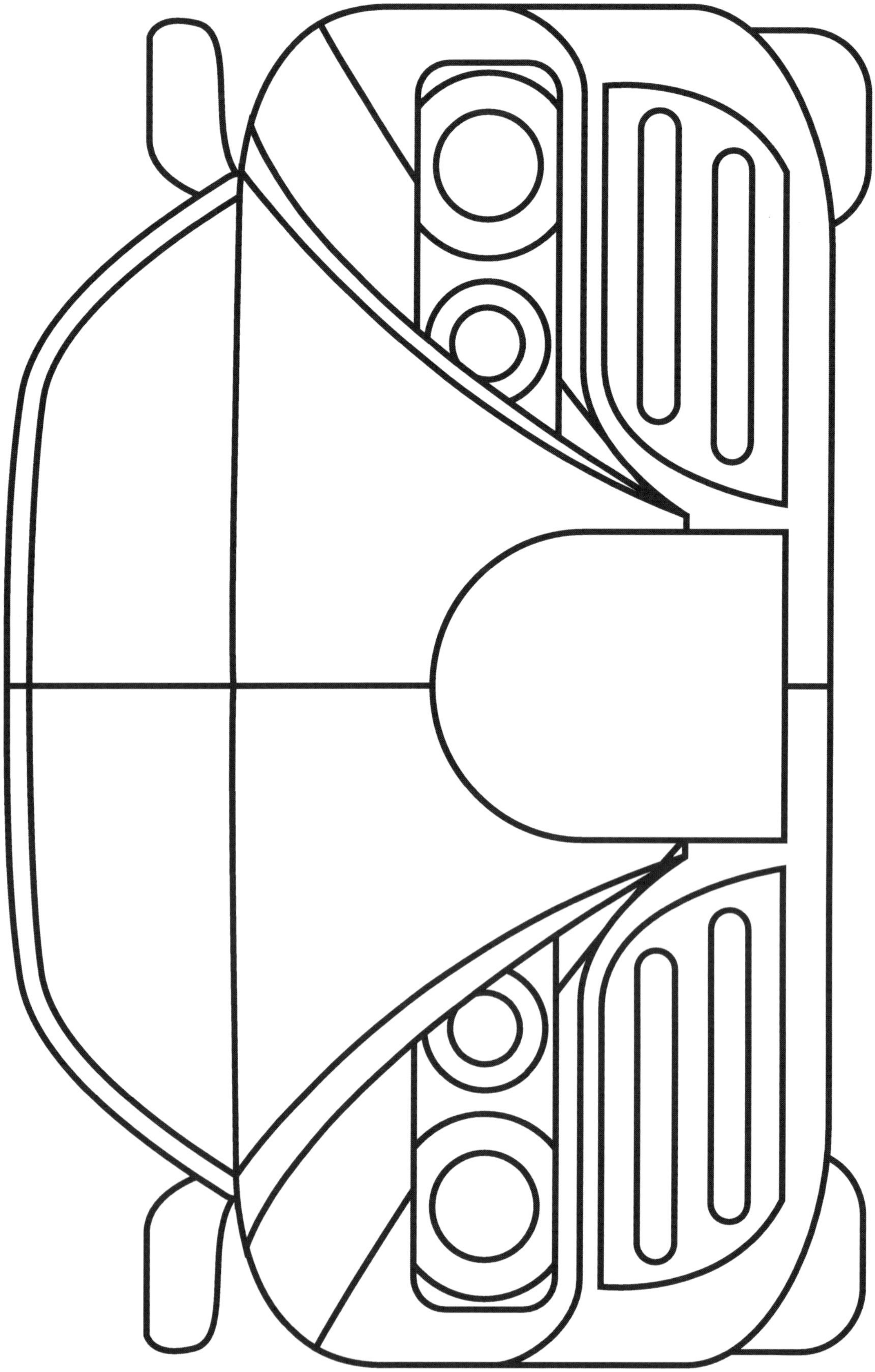

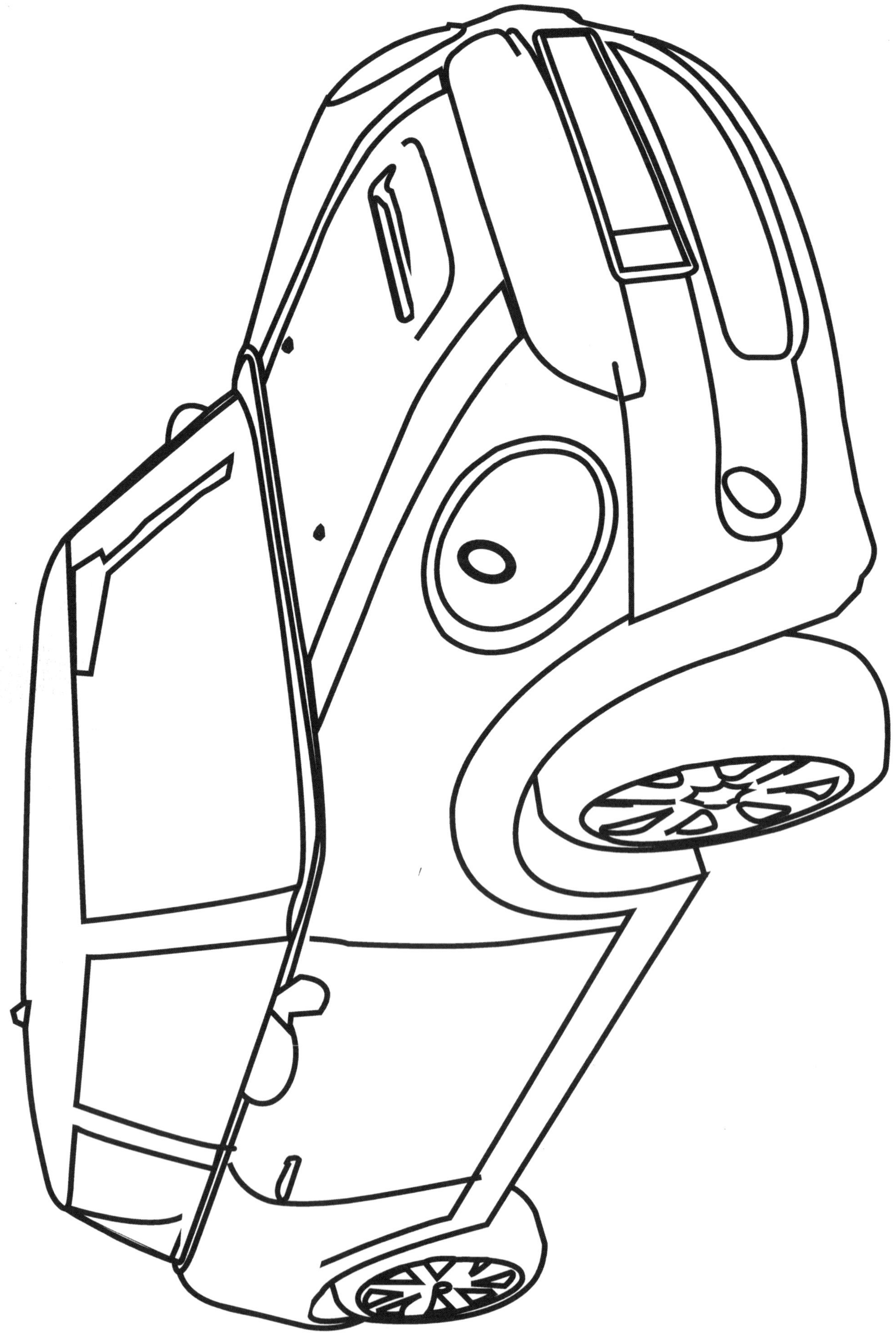

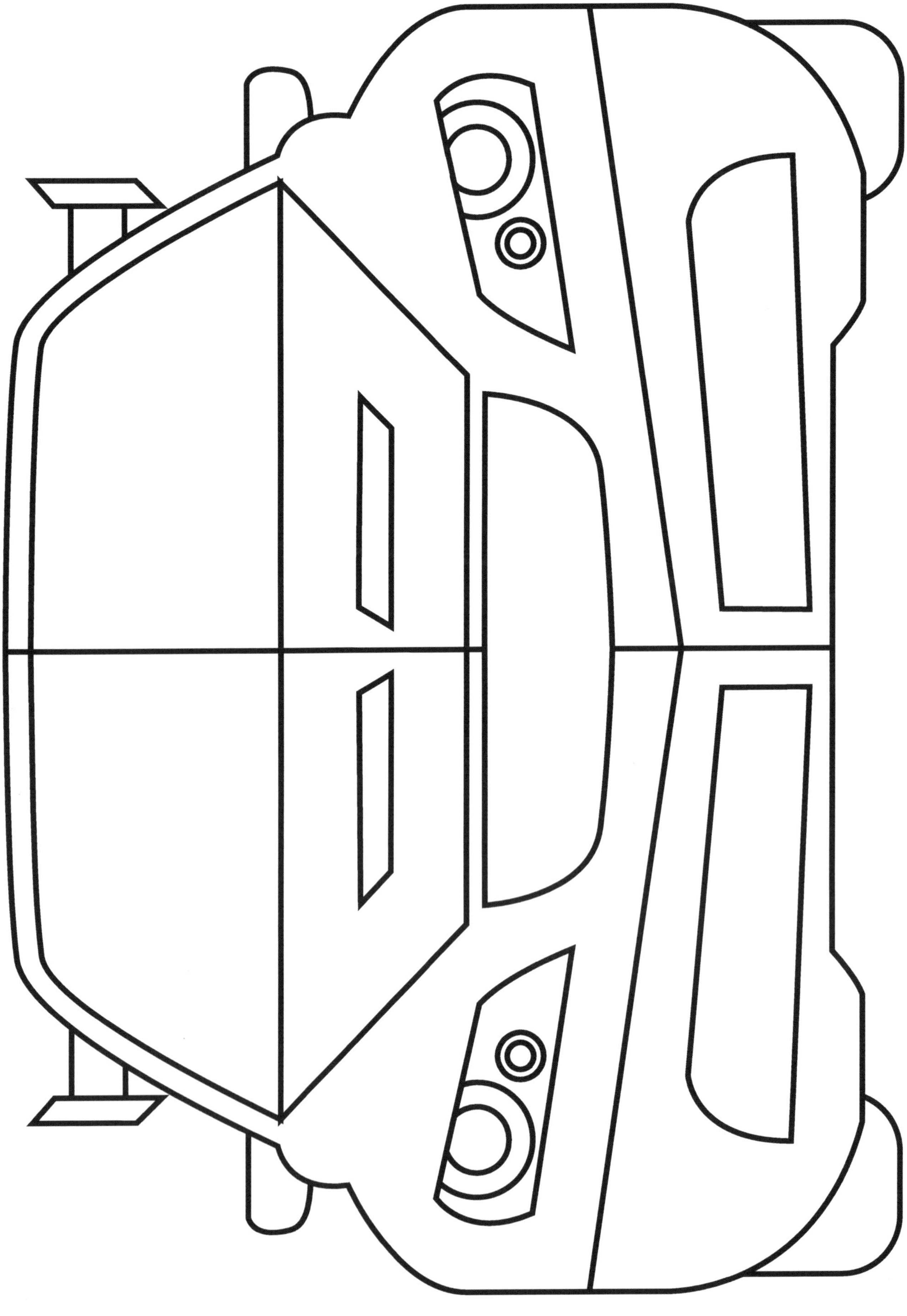

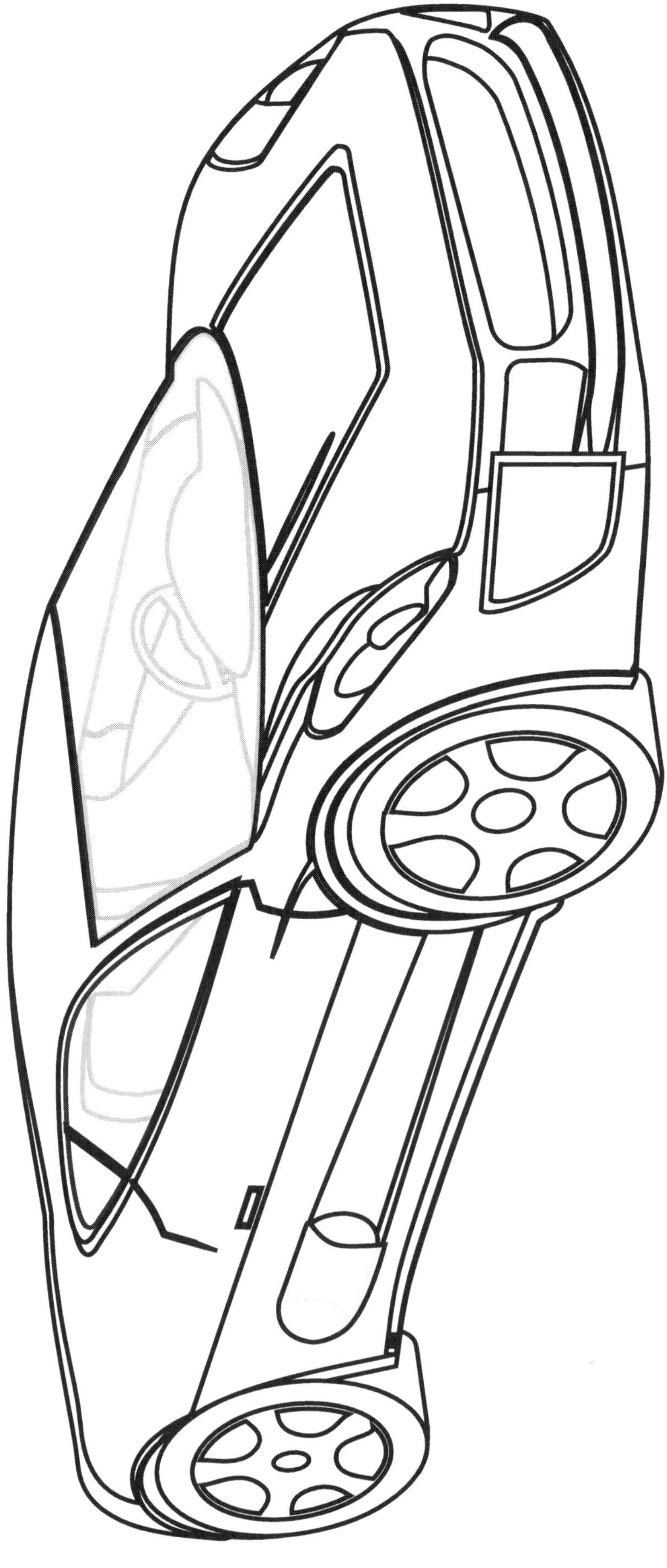

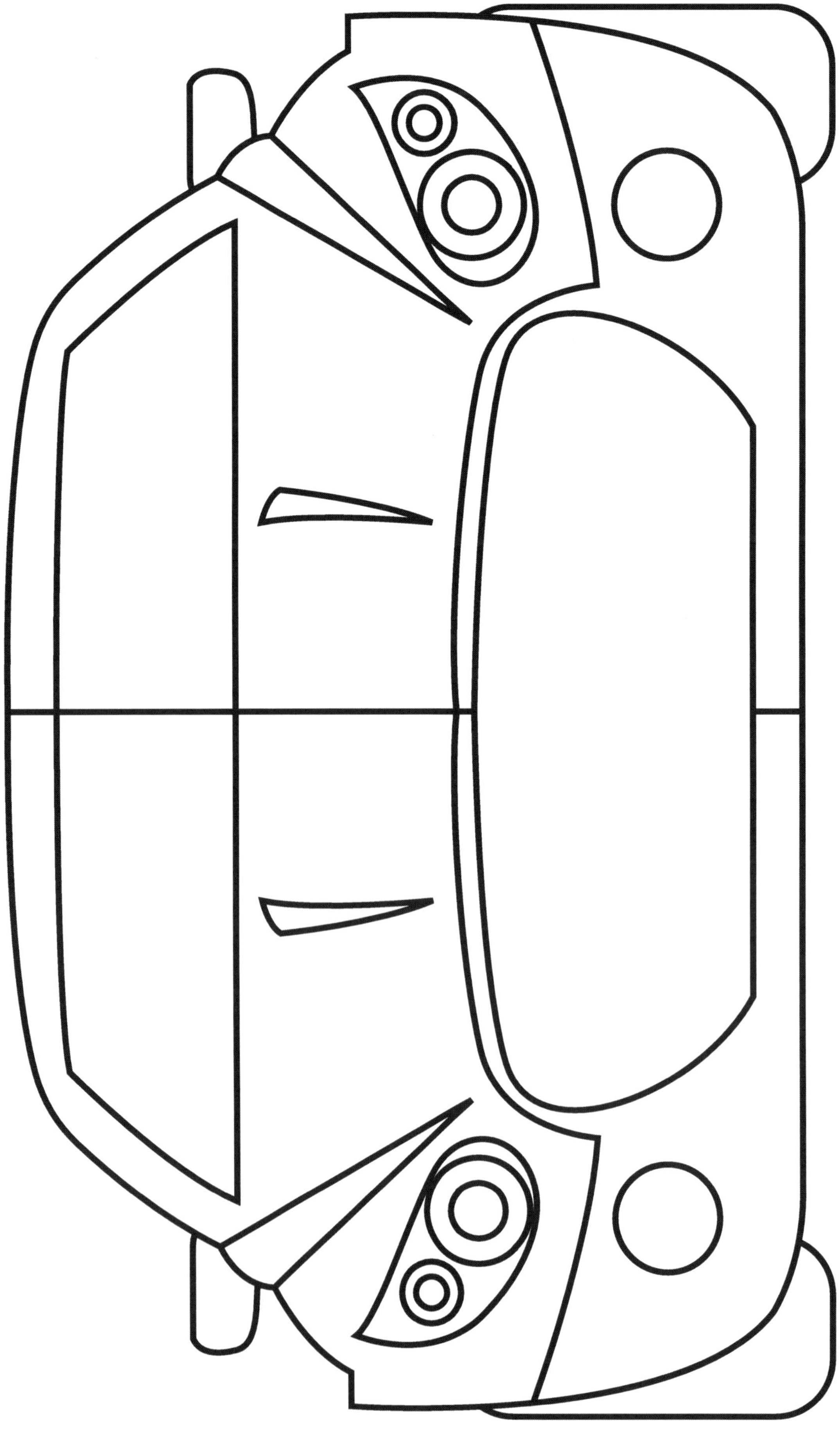

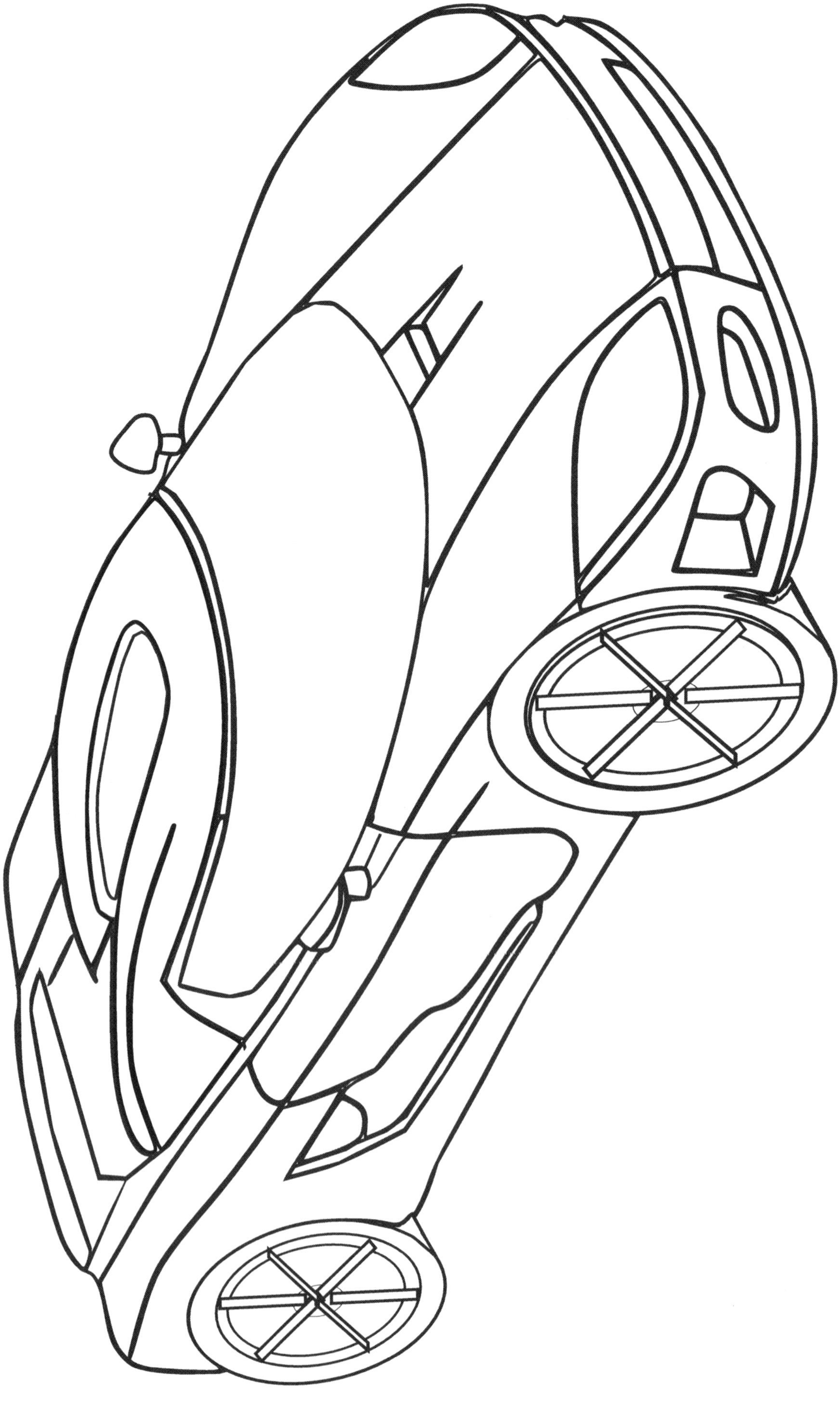

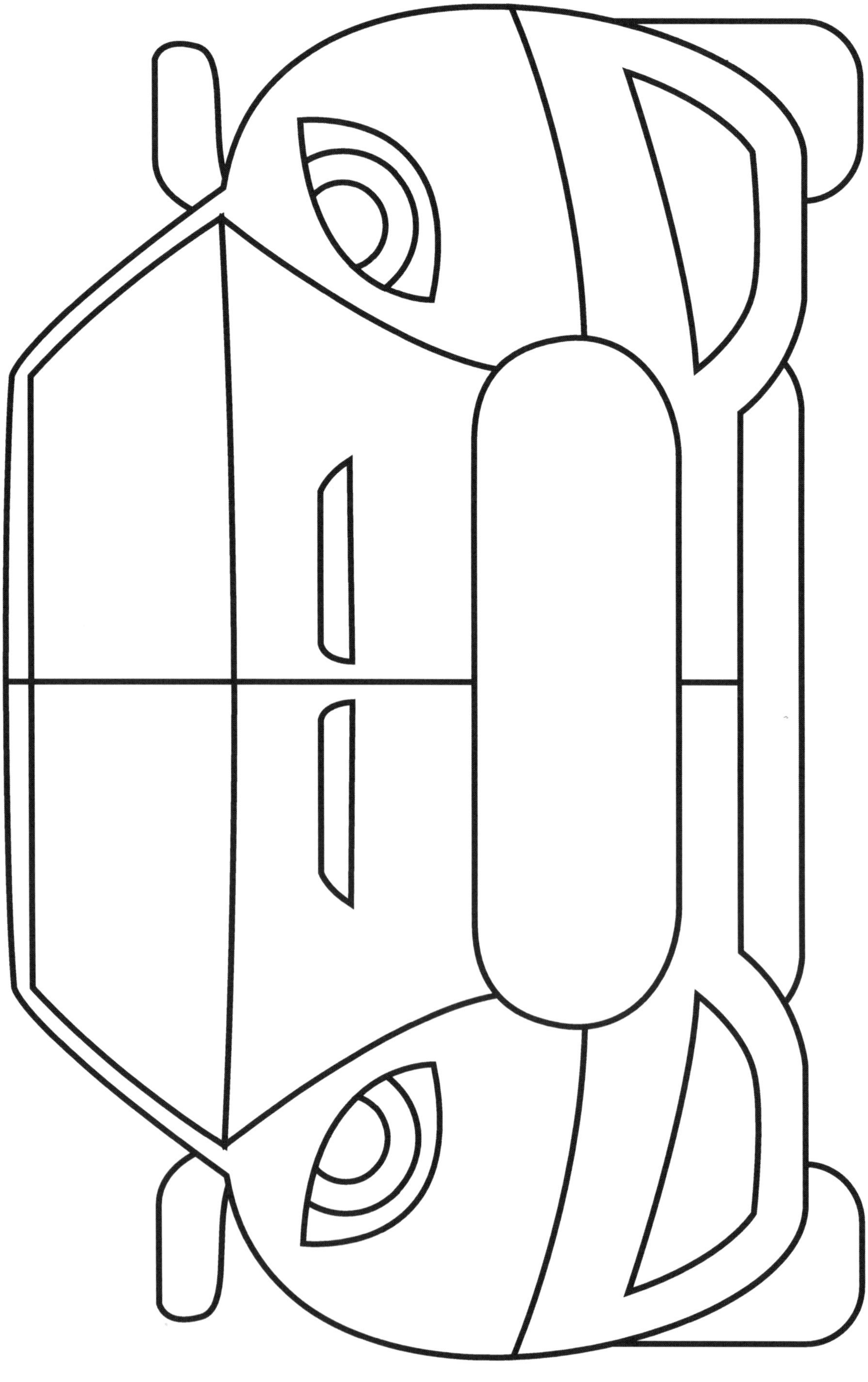

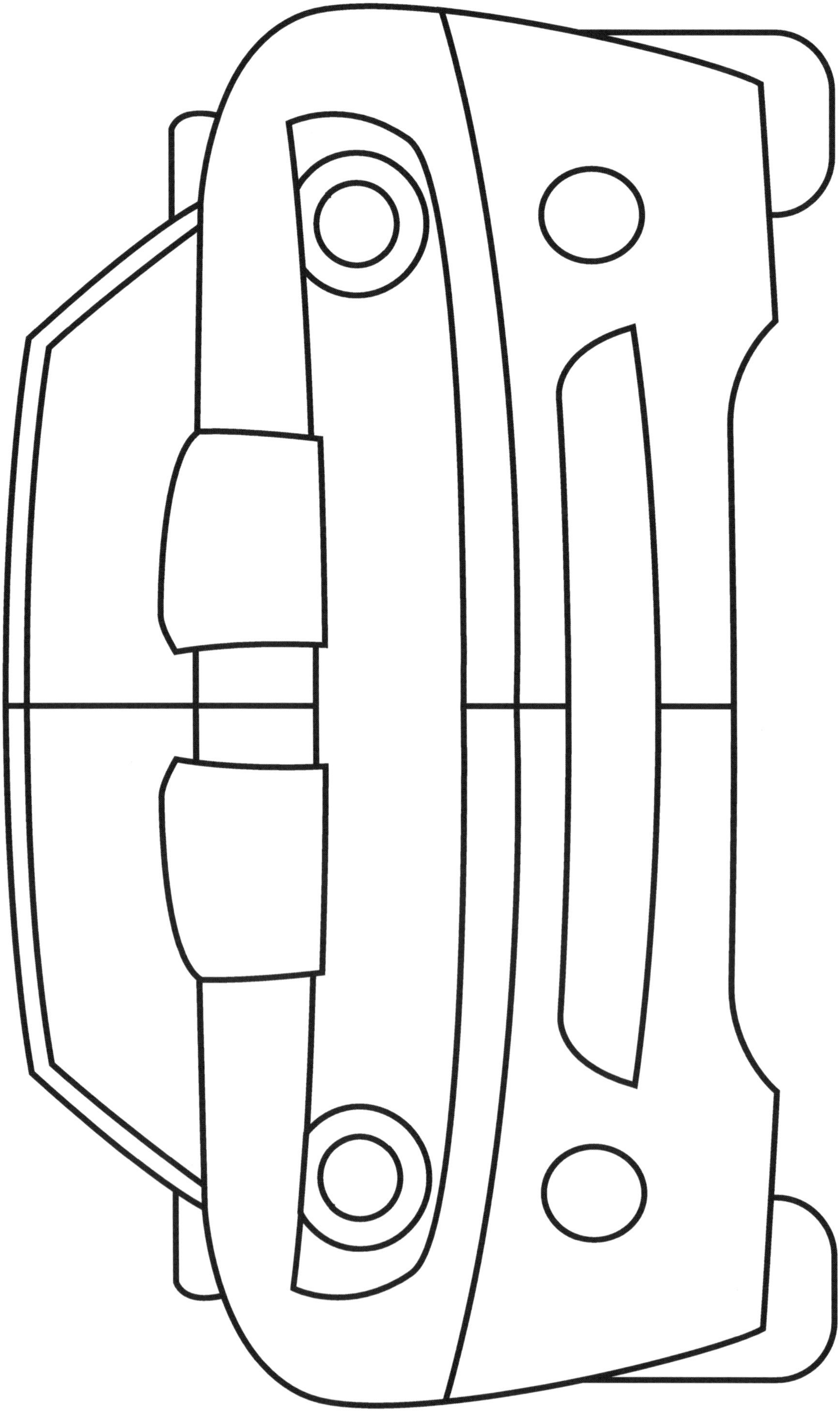

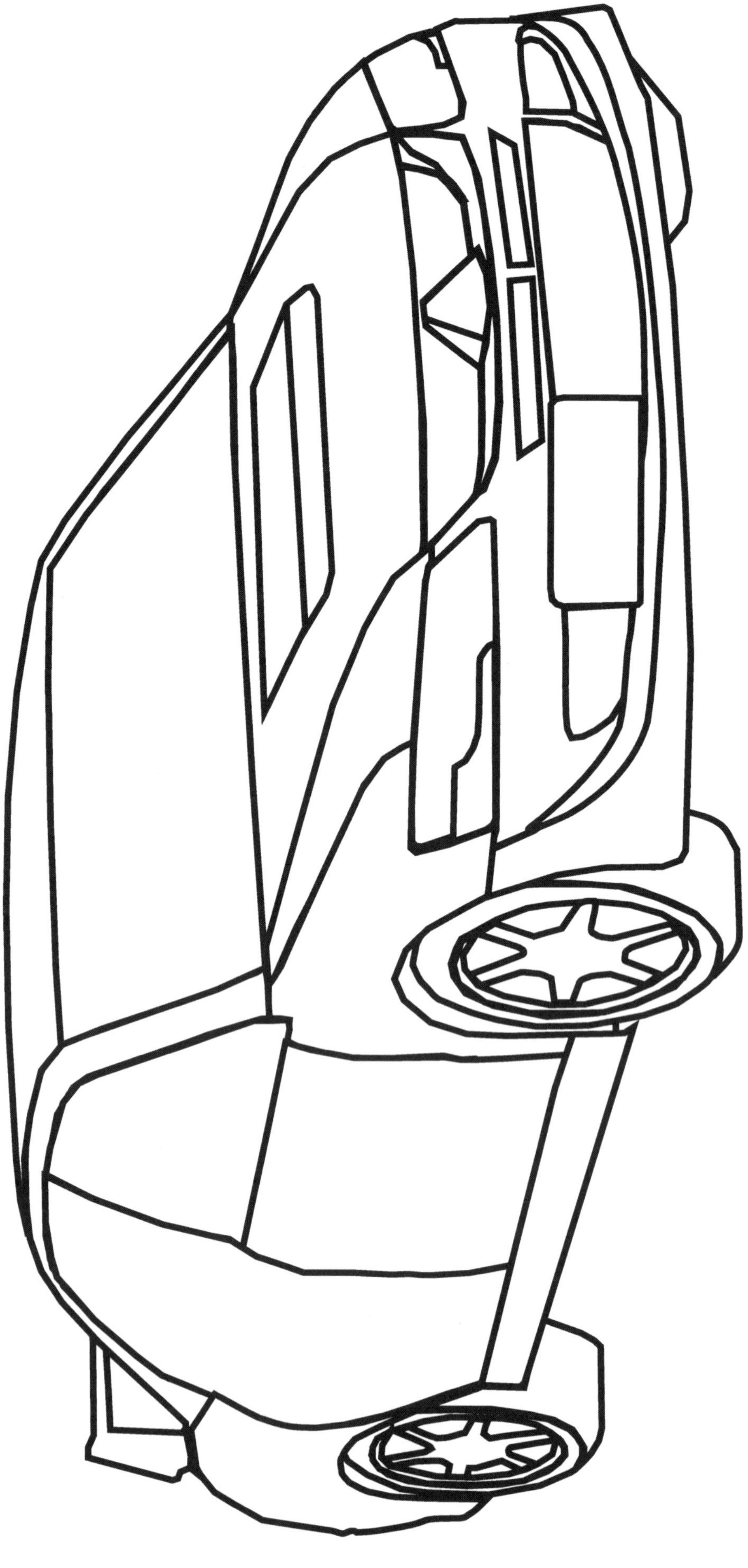

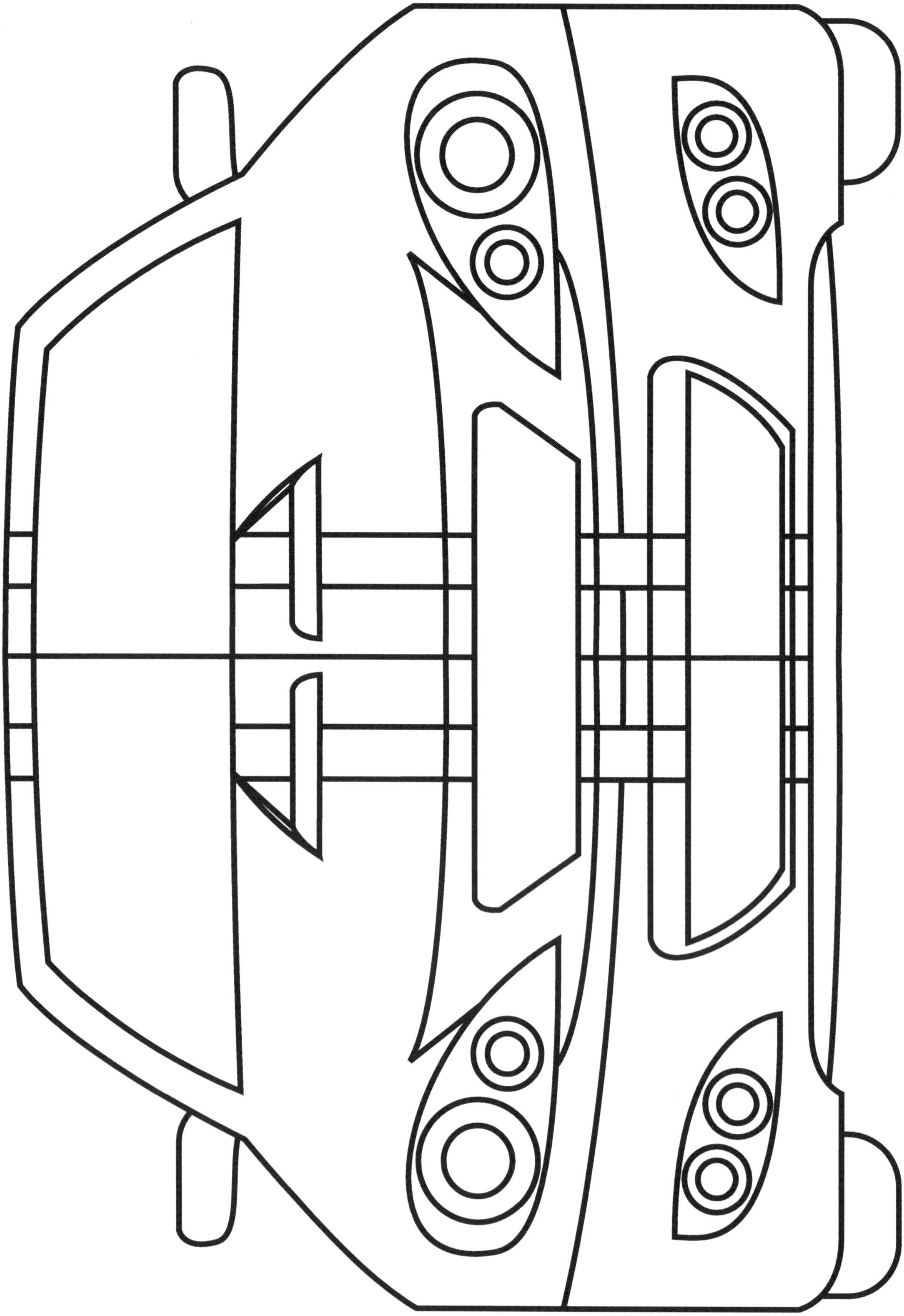

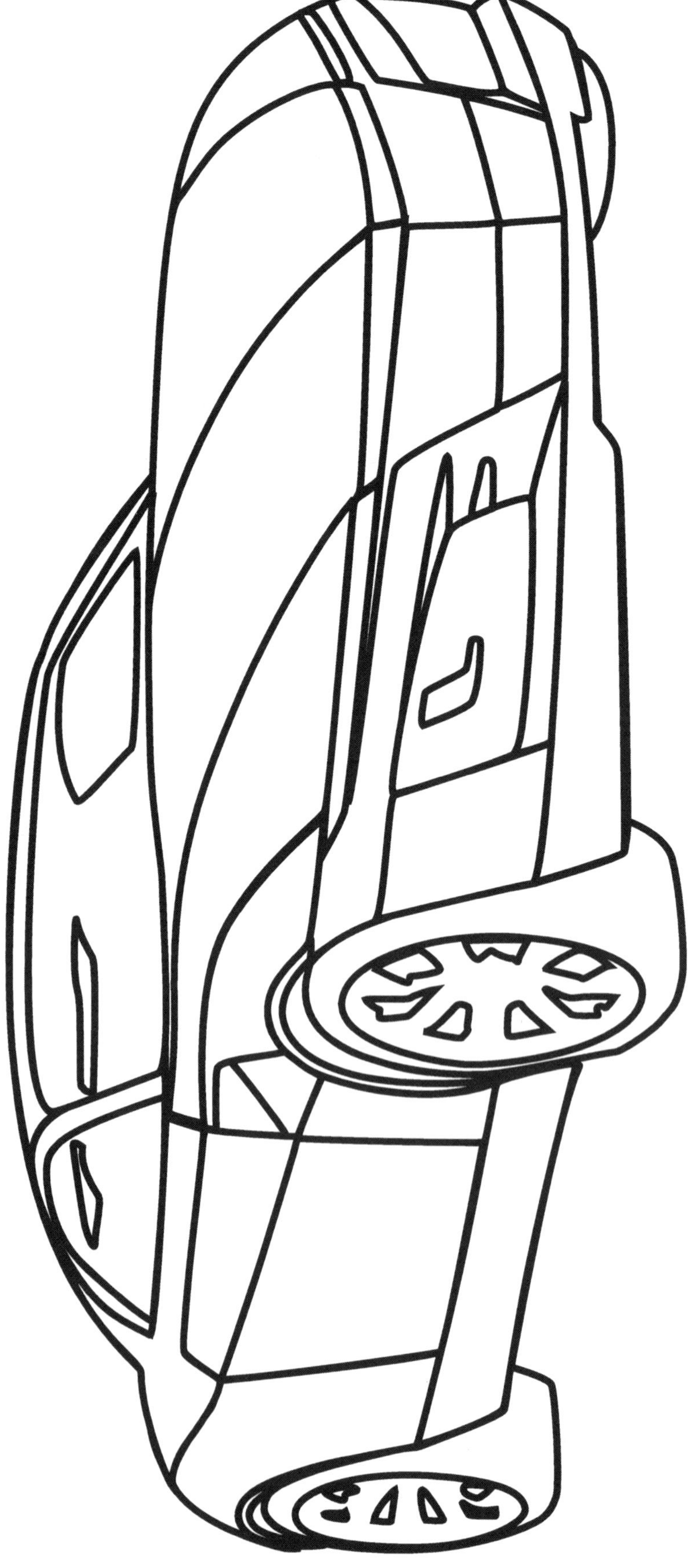

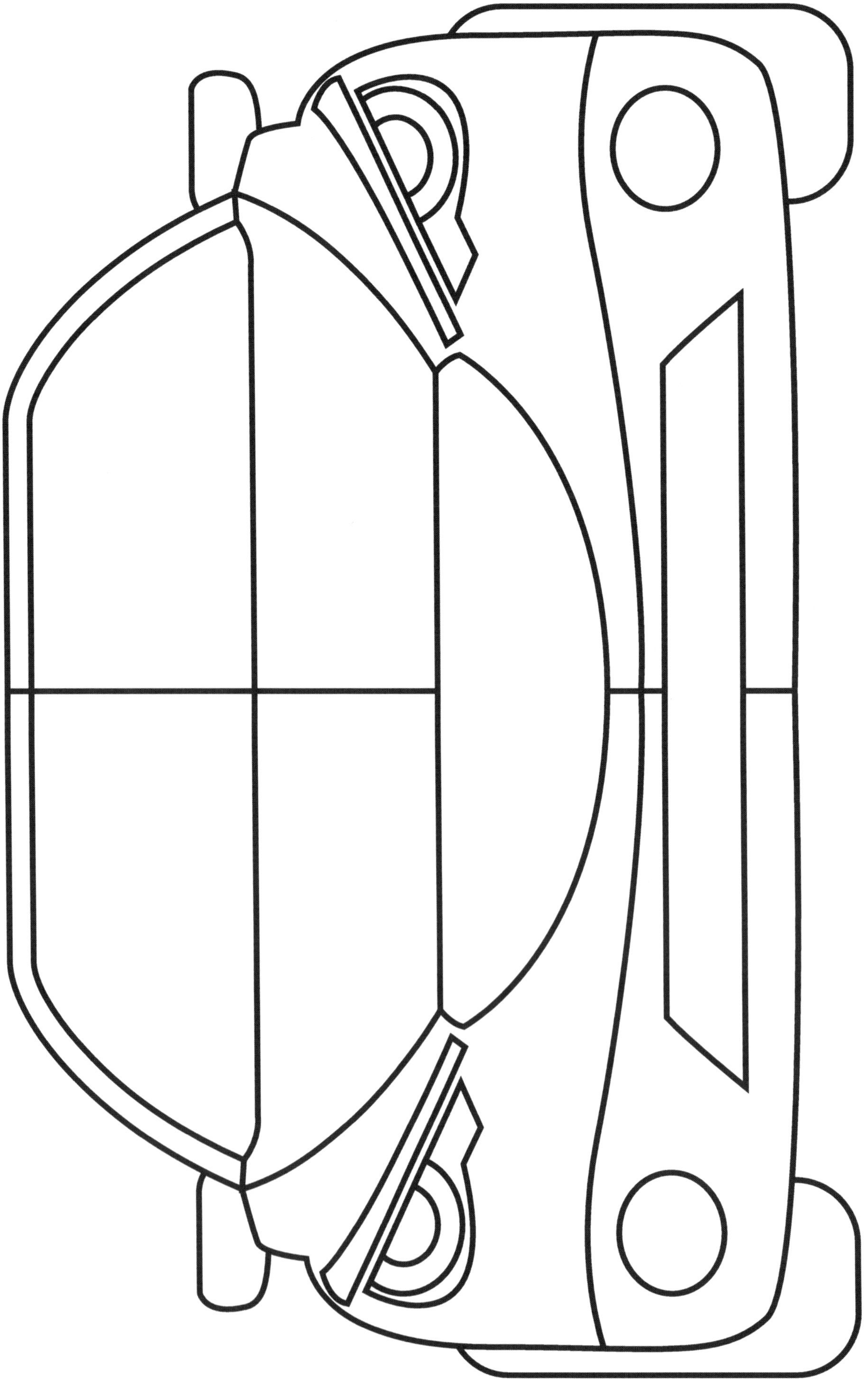

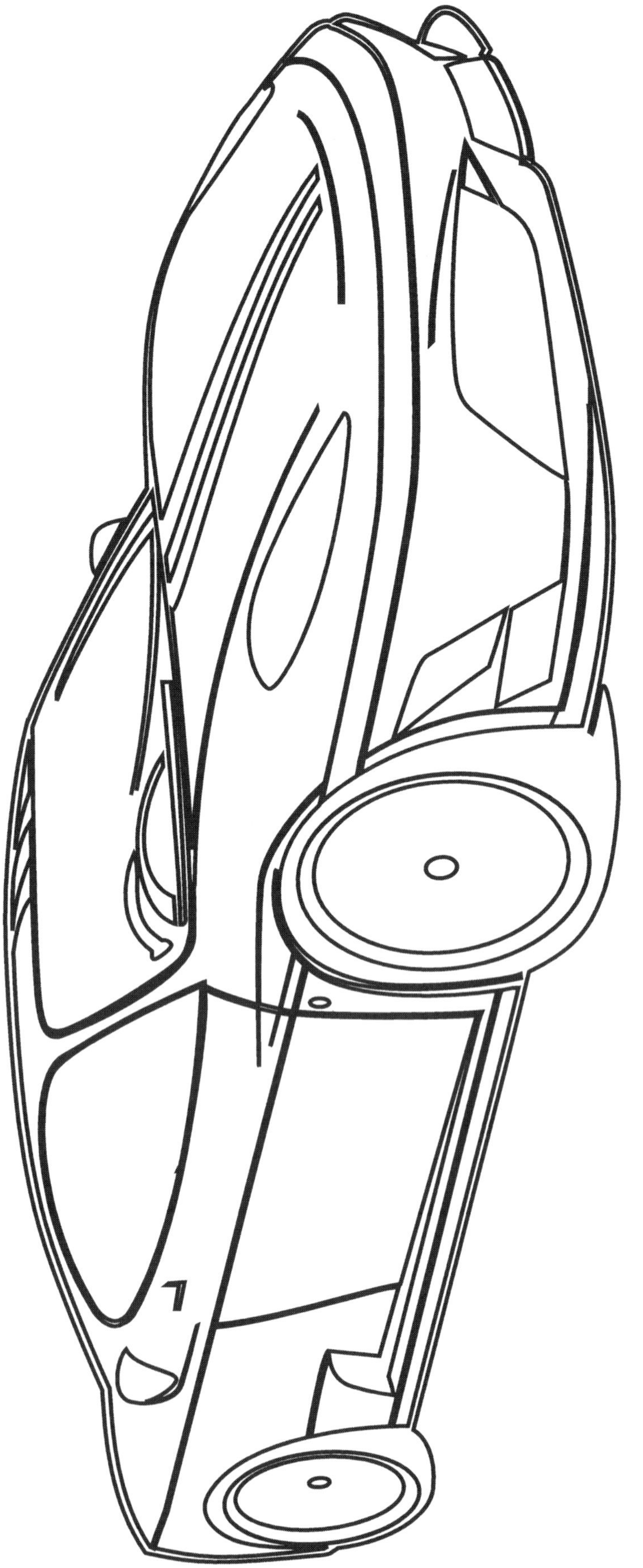

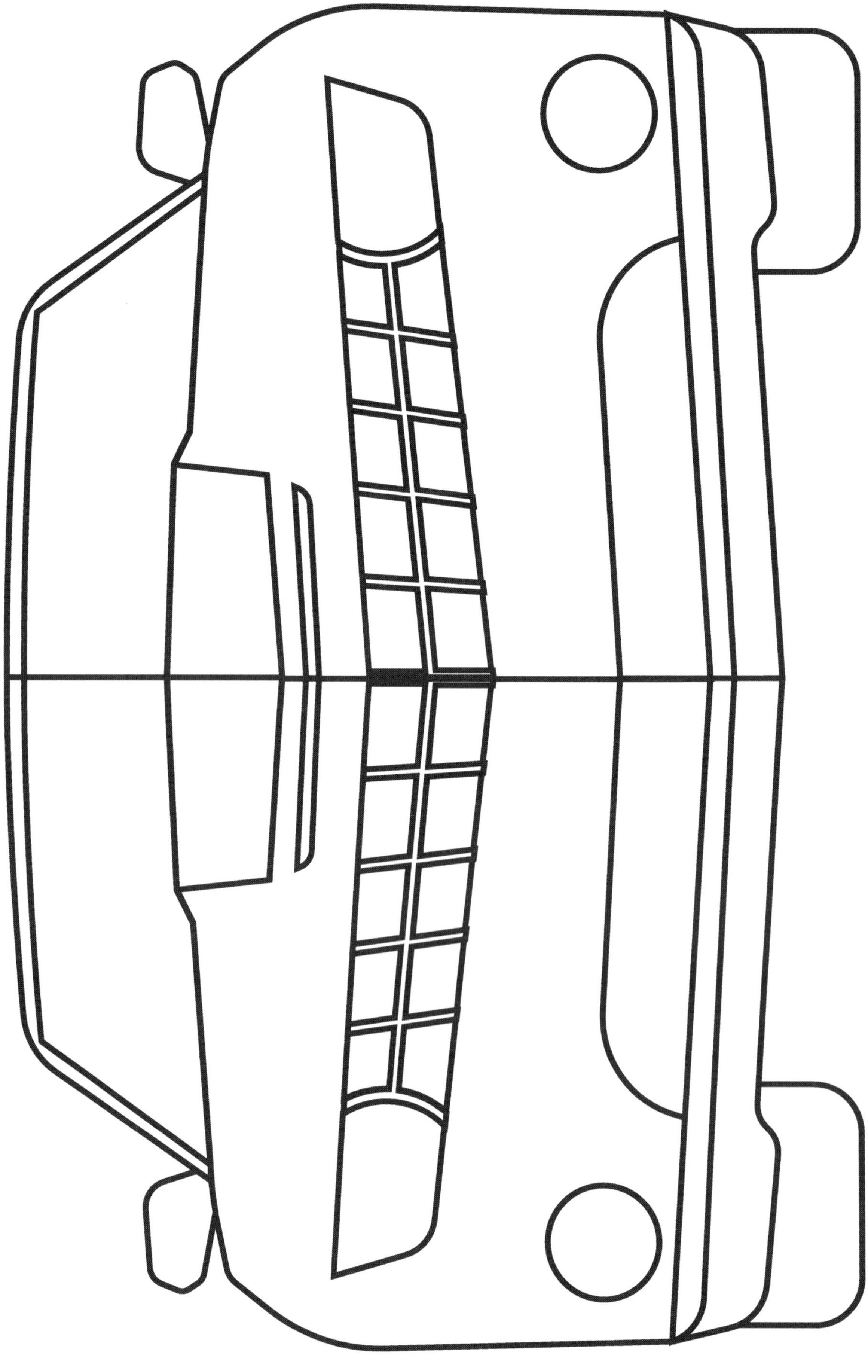

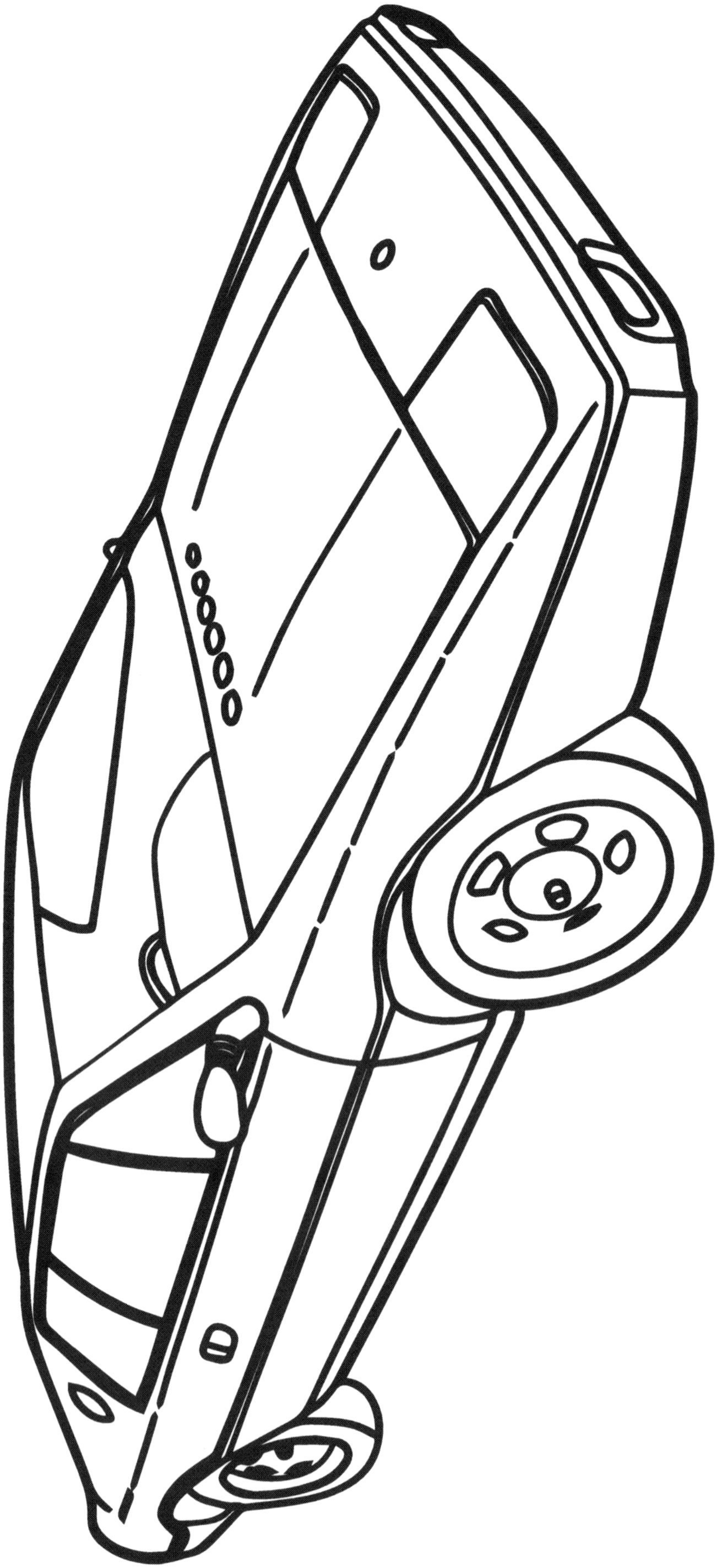

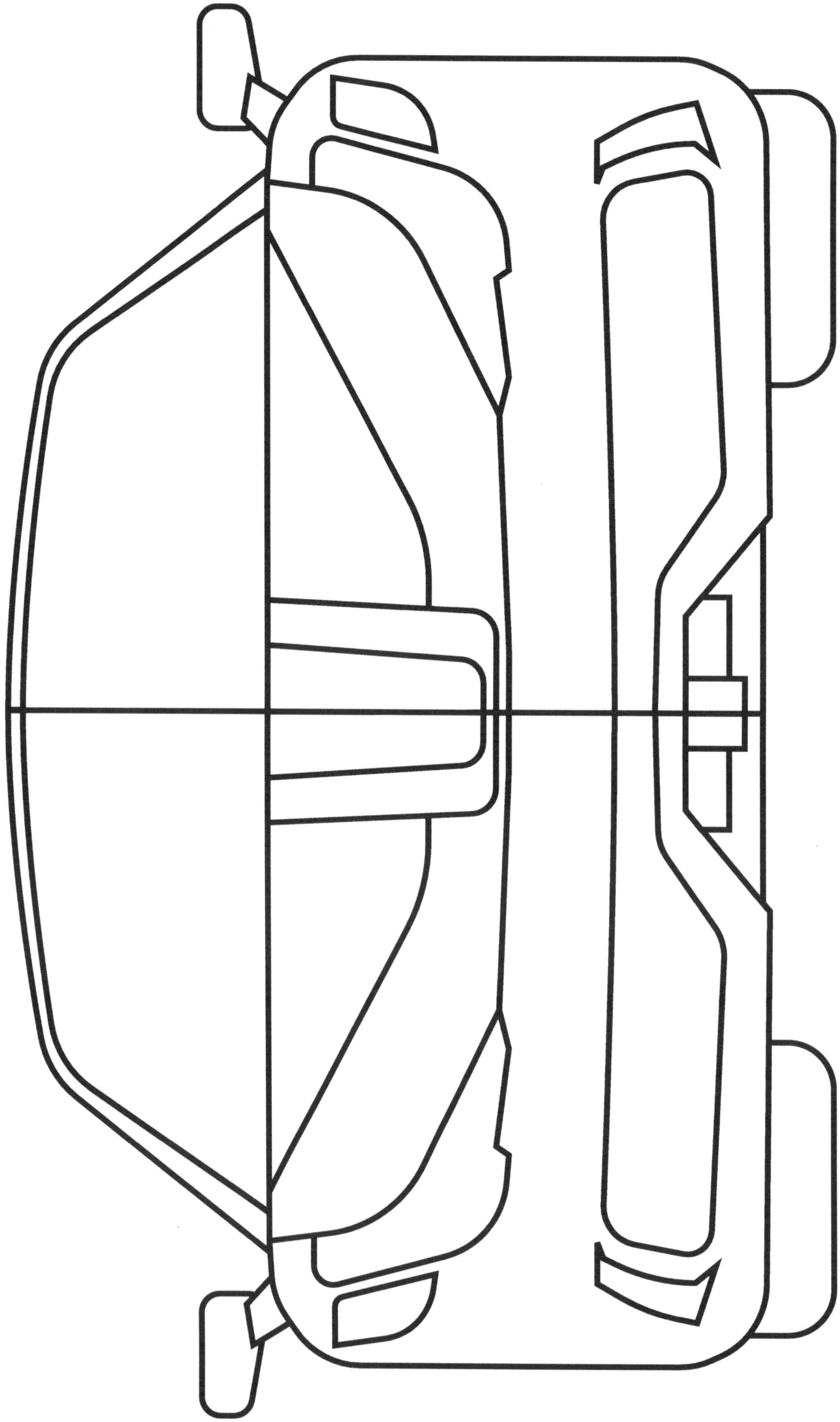

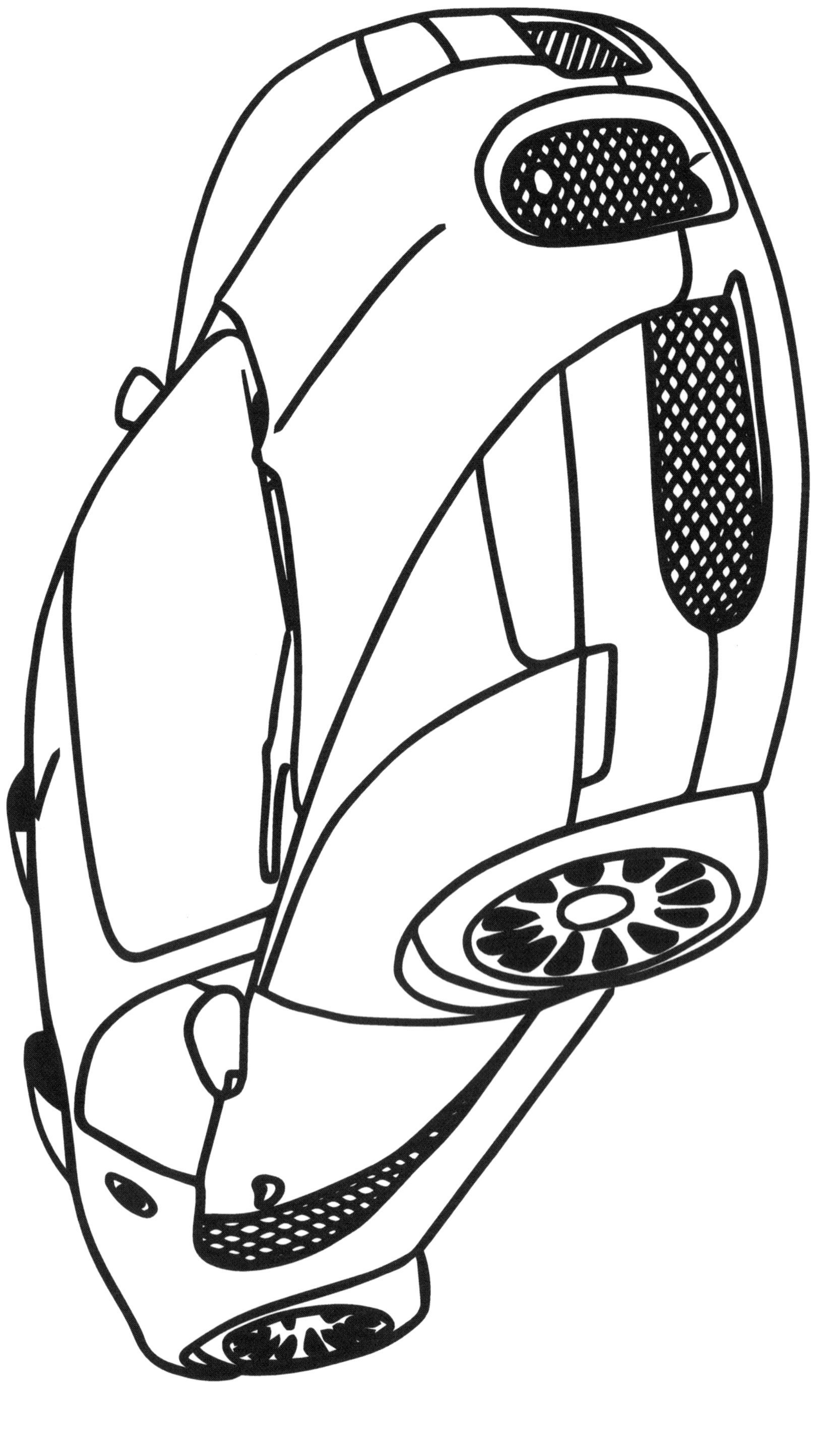

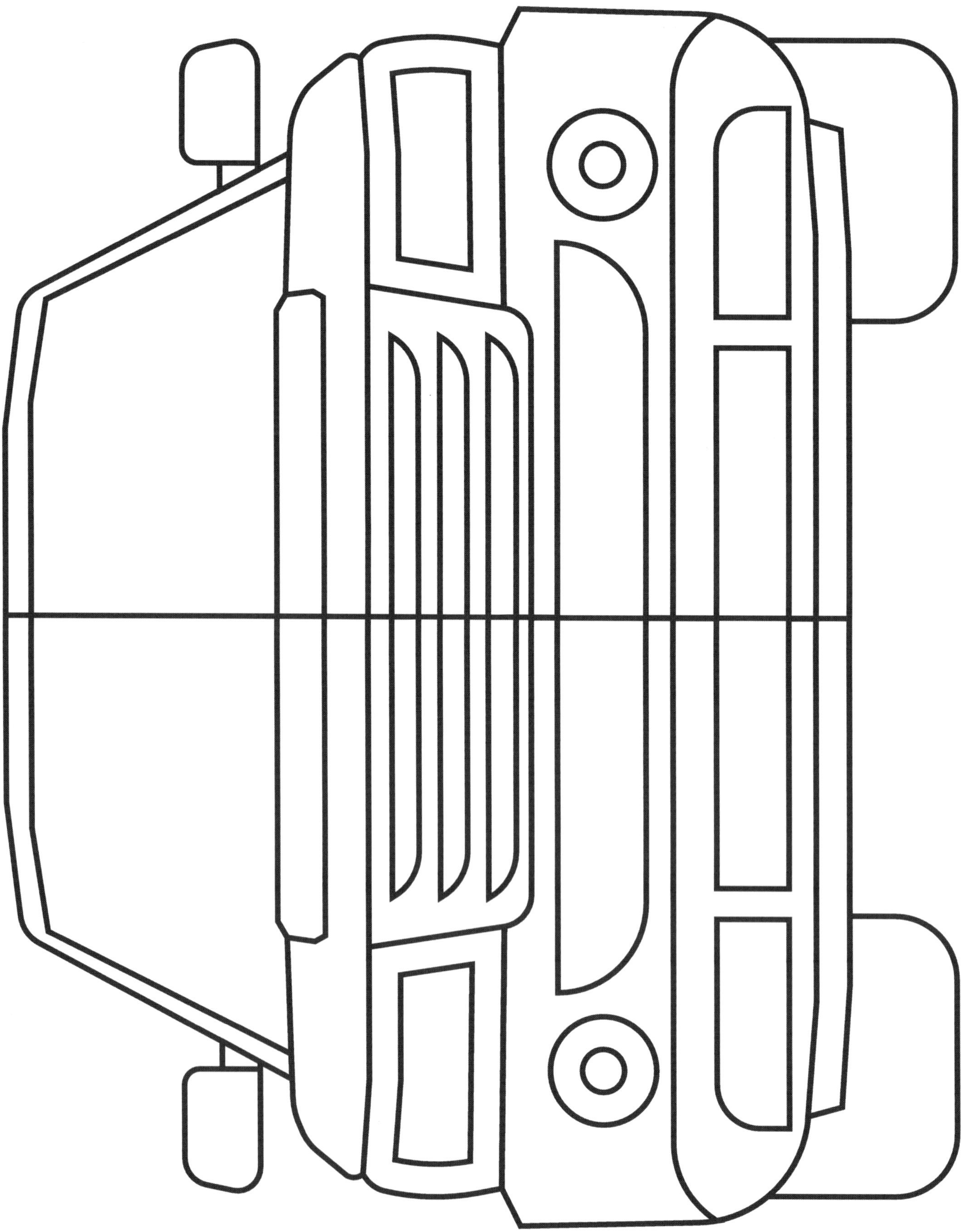

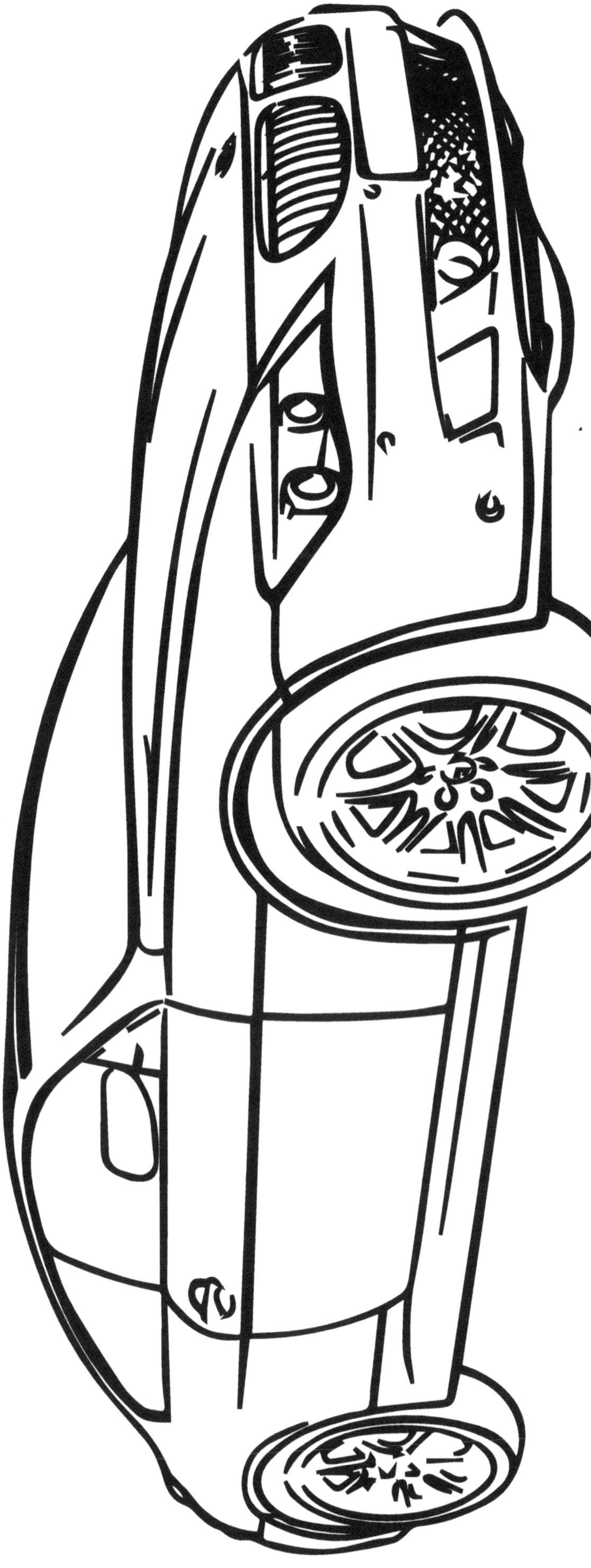

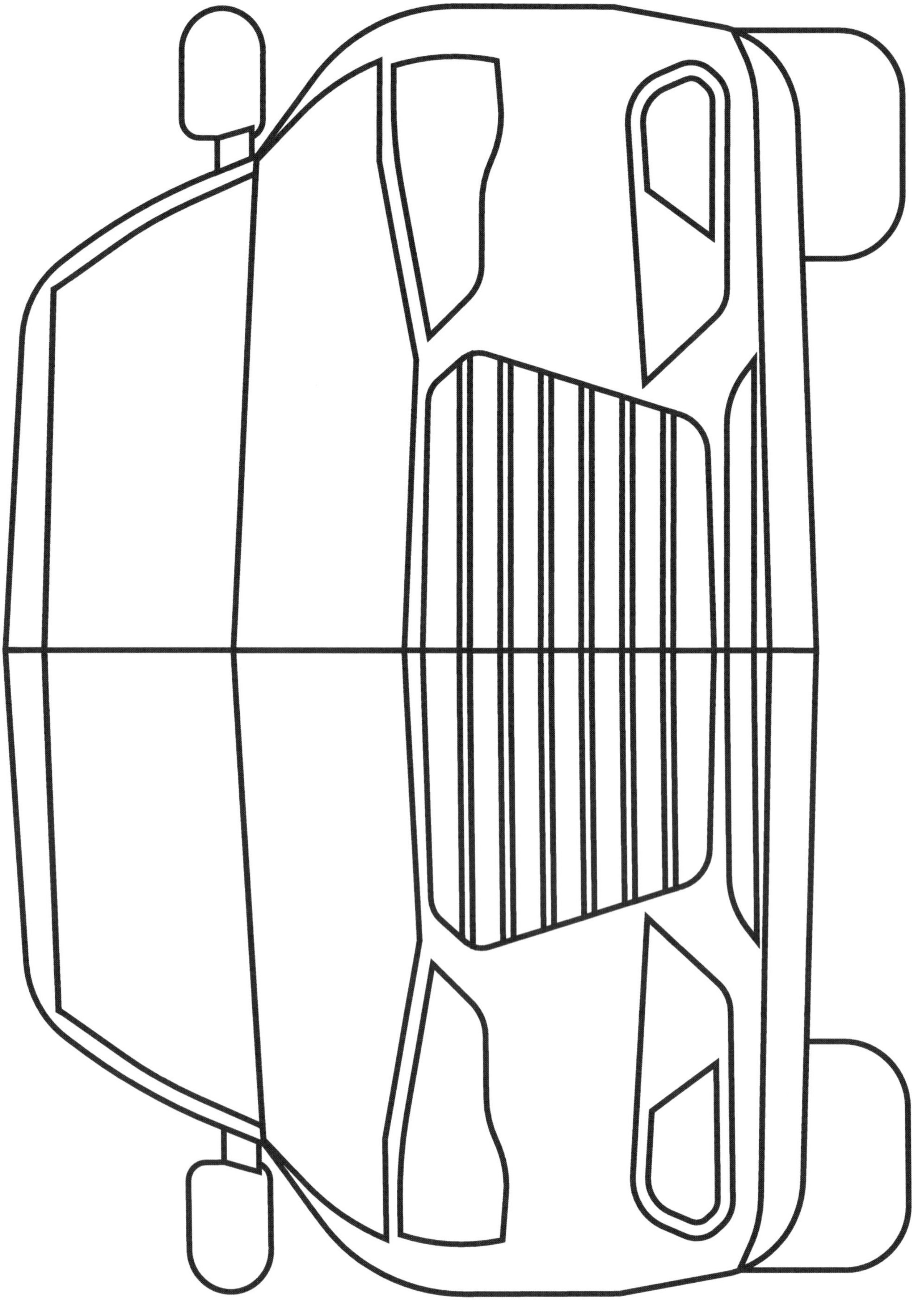

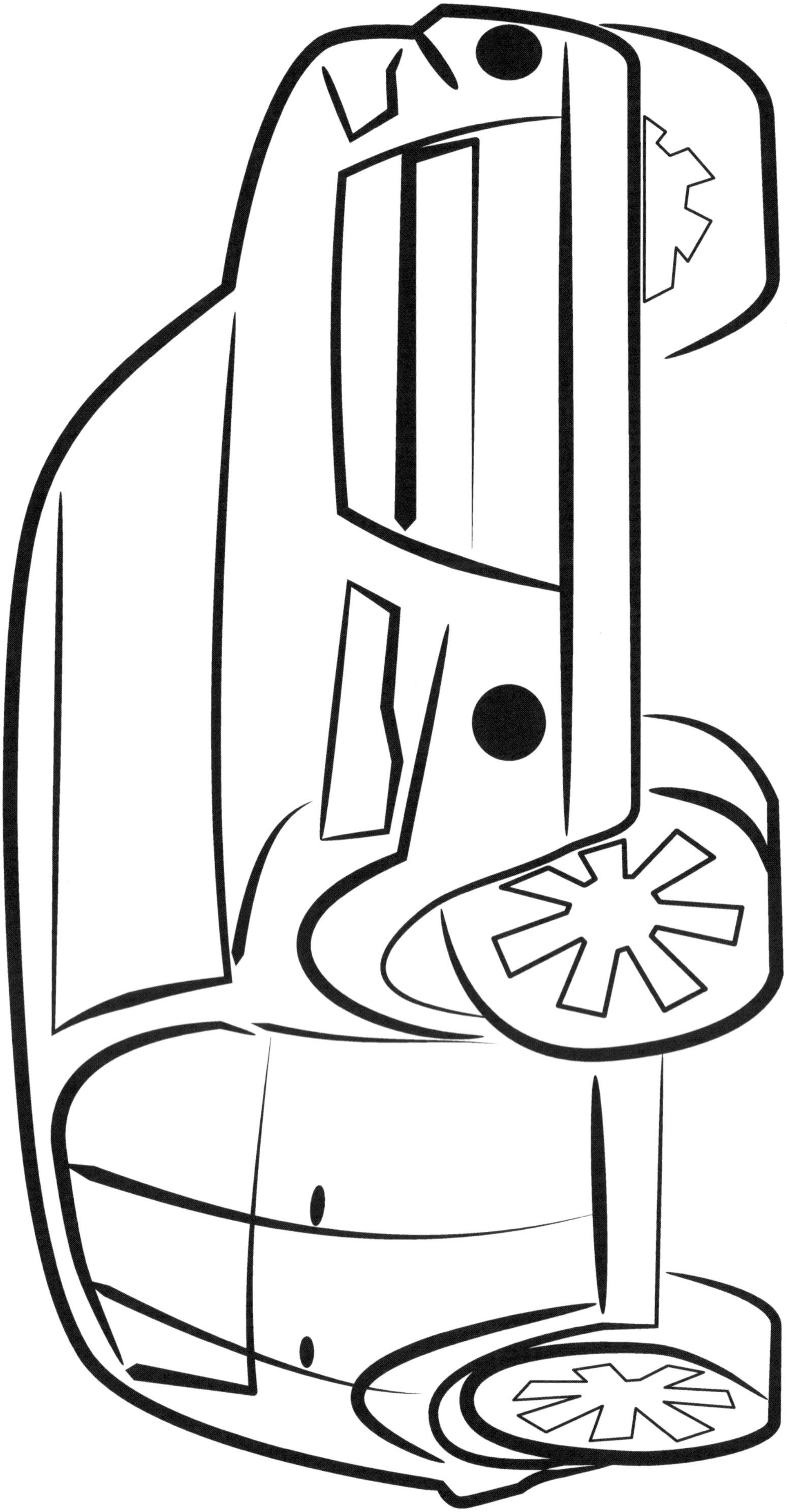

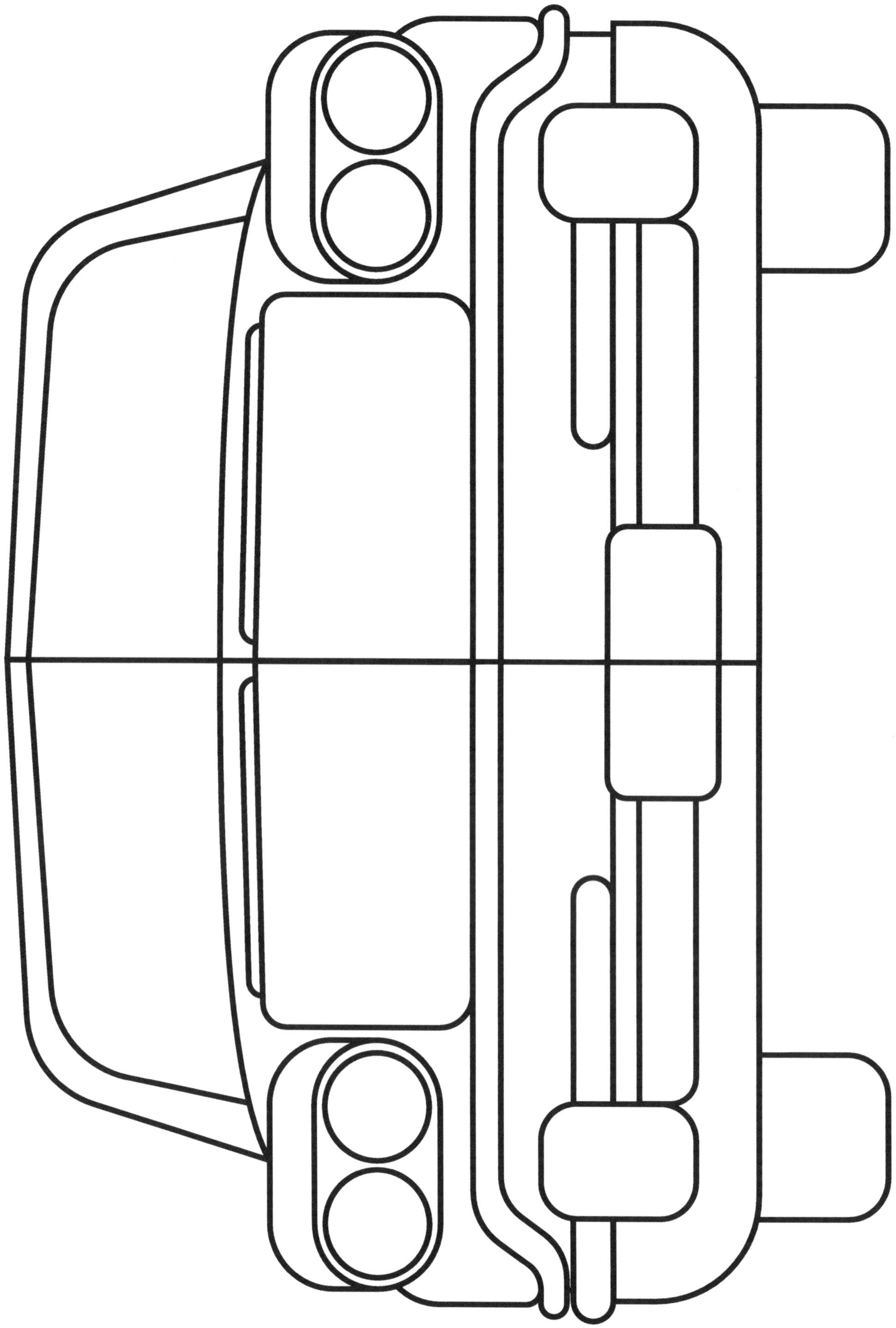

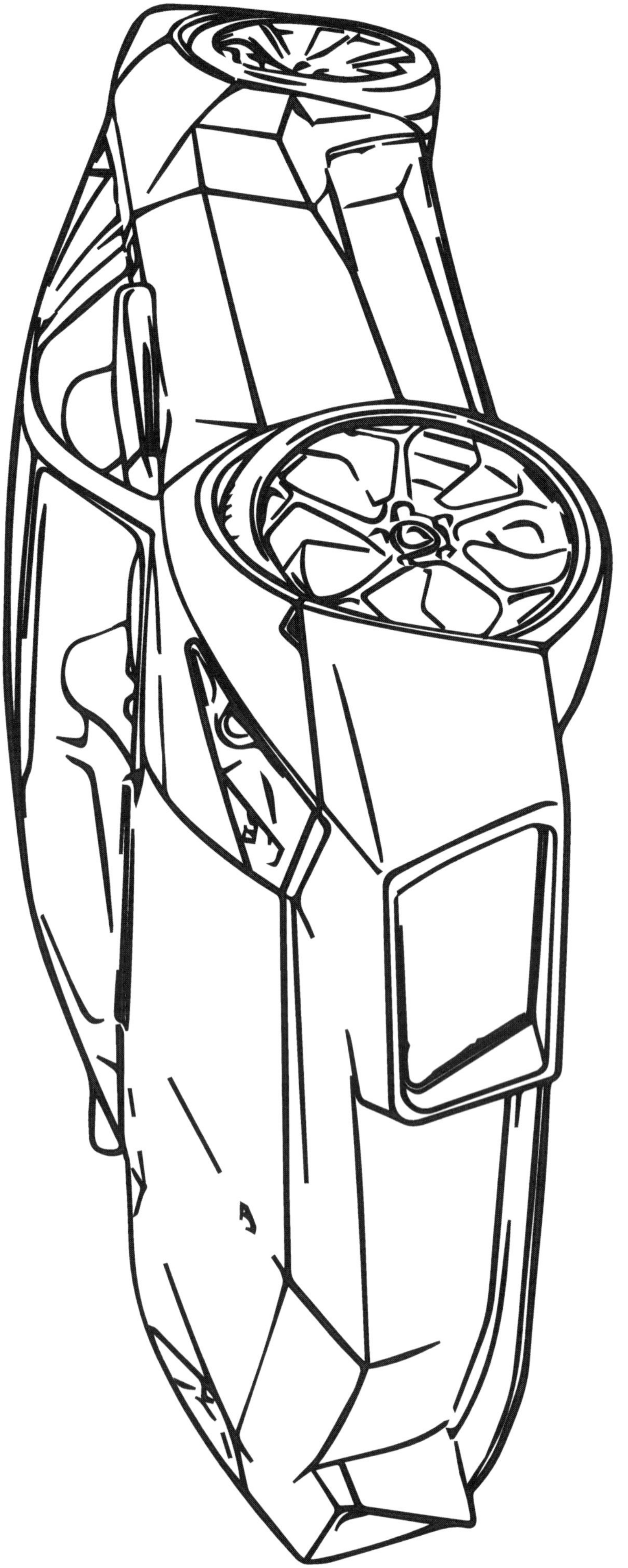

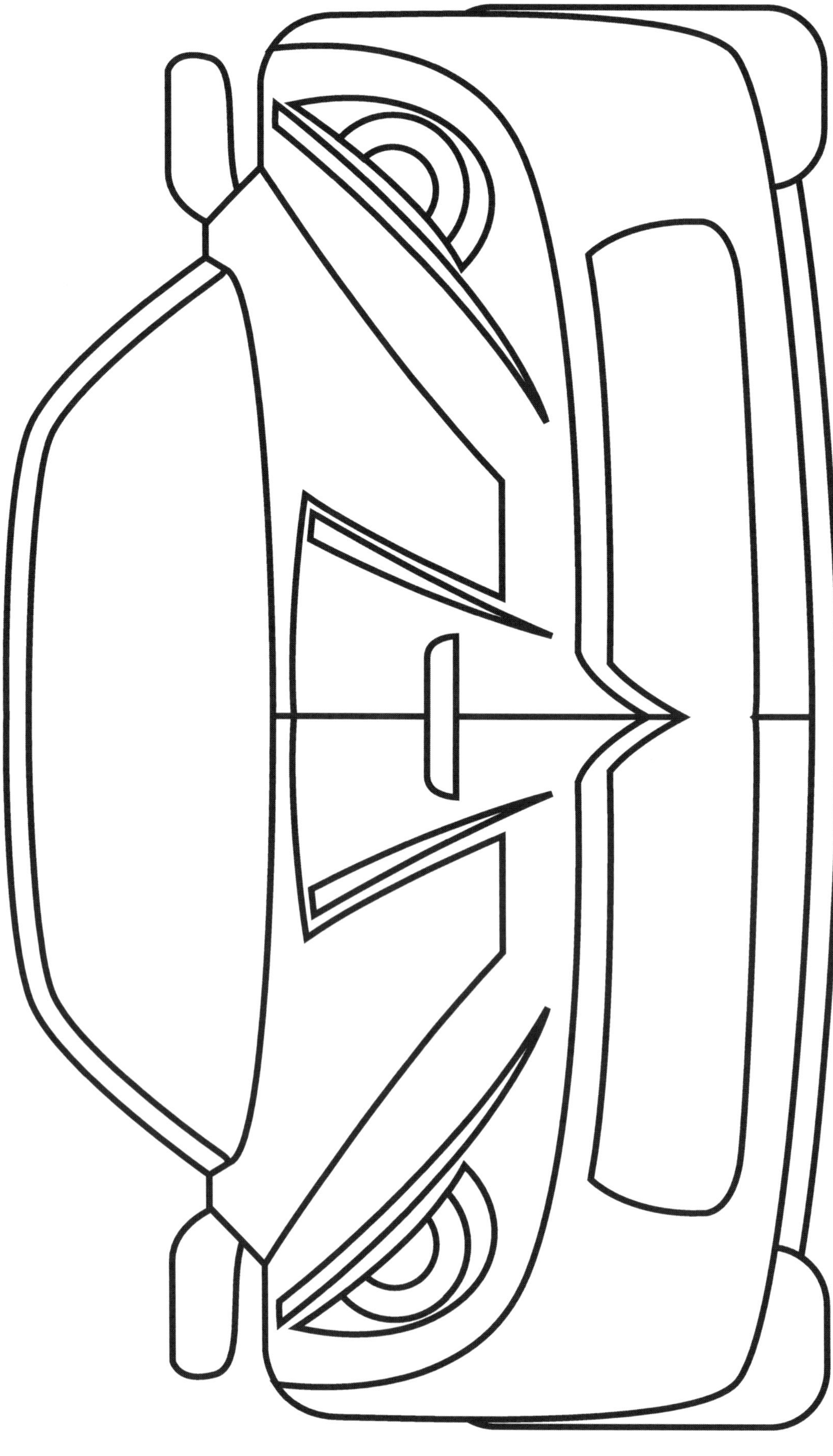

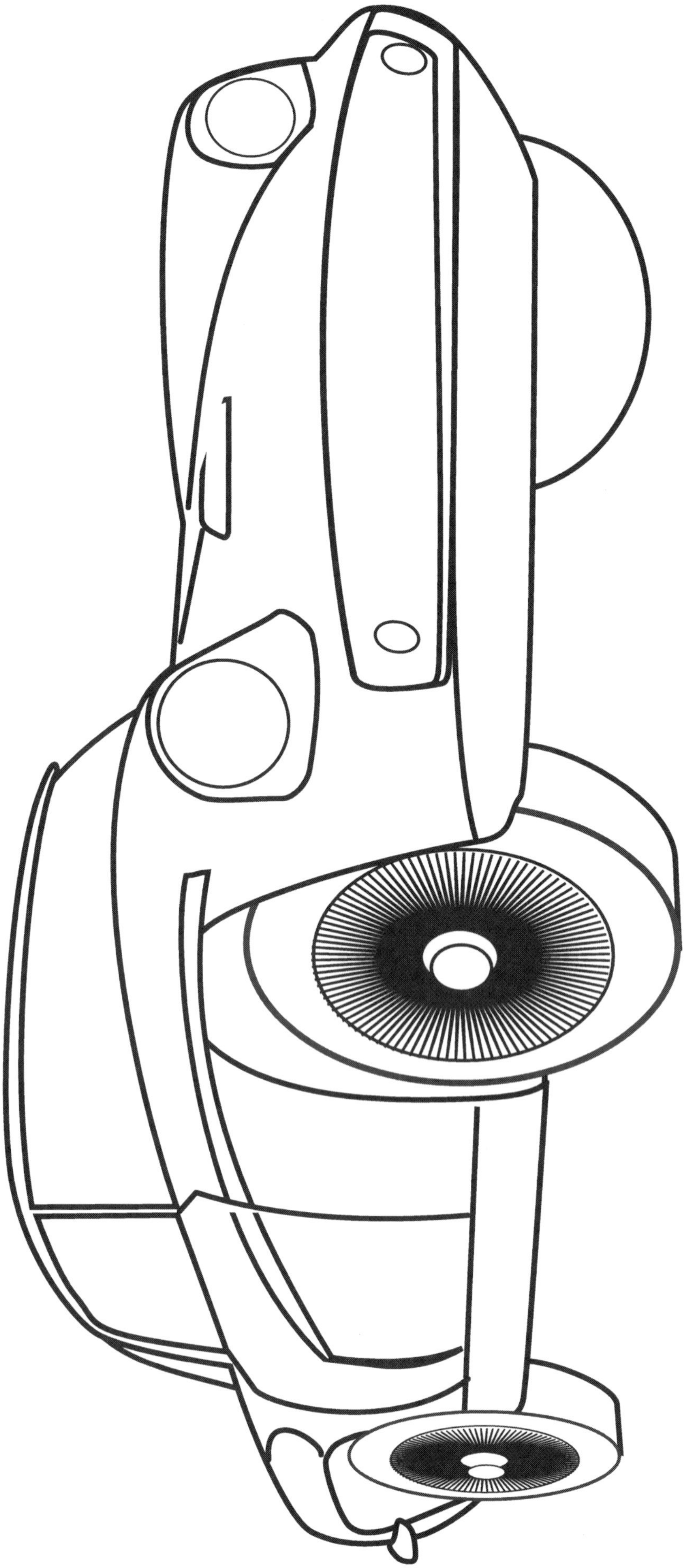

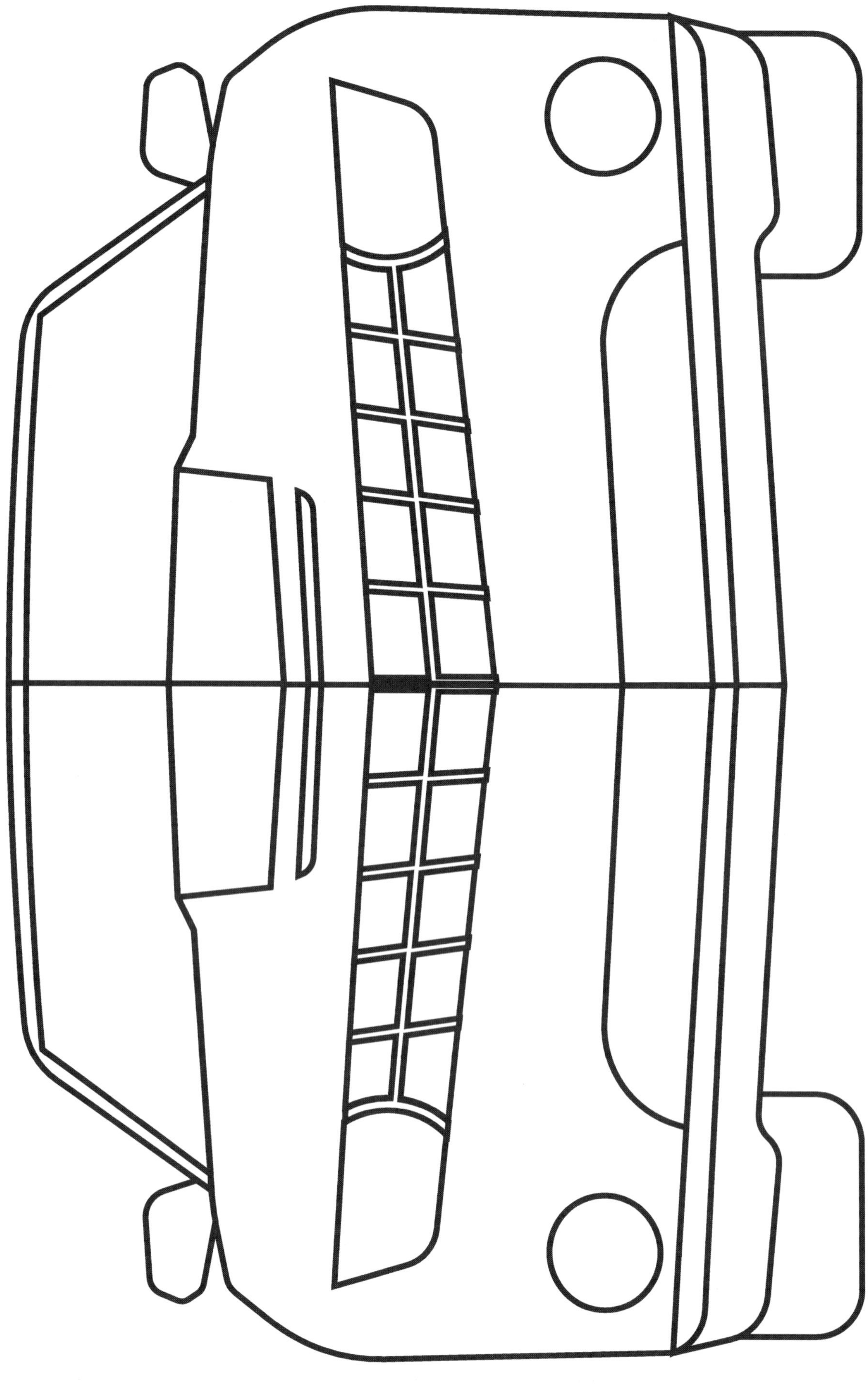

Printed in Great Britain
by Amazon

16539515R00036